PROOF REQUIRED UNDER HOMESTEAD ACTS MAY 20, 1862,

WE, *Joseph Graff* *Kilpatrick* do solemnly *swear*

that we have known *Daniel Emman* for *over five* years last past; that he

... consisting of *wife* ...he is an inhabitant

and *Two*

Fact Finders®

A Primary Source History of
WESTWARD EXPANSION

by Steven Otfinoski

Consultant: Malcolm J. Rohrbough
Professor Emeritus
Department of History
The University of Iowa

Fact Finders Books are published by Capstone Press,
1710 Roe Crest Drive, North Mankato, Minnesota 56003
www.capstonepub.com

Library of Congress Cataloging-in-Publication Data
Otfinoski, Steven.
A primary source history of Westward expansion / by Steven Otfinoski.
pages cm. — (Fact finders. Primary source history)
Summary: "Uses primary sources to tell the story of Westward Expansion in the
United States"— Provided by publisher.
Includes bibliographical references and index.
ISBN 978-1-4914-1841-3 (library binding) — ISBN 978-1-4914-1845-1 (pbk.) —
ISBN 978-1-4914-1849-9 (ebook pdf)
1. United States—Territorial expansion—Juvenile literature. 2. West (U.S.)—History—Juvenile
literature. 3. West (U.S.)—Discovery and exploration—Juvenile literature. I. Title.
E179.5.O85 2015
978'.02—dc23   2014026741

Editorial Credits
Jennifer Besel, editor; Kyle Grenz, designer; Wanda Winch, media researcher;
    Kathy McColley, production specialist

Photo Credits
Bridgeman Images/Peter Newark American Pictures/Private Collection, 29; Capstone, 21 (top);
Corbis: Bettmann, cover (bottom), 15, James L. Amos, 17 (b); Courtesy of George Eastman House,
International Museum of Photography and Film, 23; CriaImages.com/Jay Robert Nash Collection,
5, 13; Getty Images: Fotosearch, 22, 26; Jim Carson, jimcarsonstudio.com, 7 (t), 9, 17 (t); Library
of Congress: Prints and Photographs Collection, 1 (b), 25, 27, Rare Books and Special Collections
Division, 11, 21 (b); National Archives and Record Administration (NARA): Homestead Act, Public
Law 37-64, 05/20/1862. Record Group 11; General Records of the U.S. Government, cover (t), 1 (t),
24; North Wind Picture Archives, 6 (b); Tales of the Day ©Heide Presse, 19; The University of Texas
at Austin/Dolph Briscoe Center for American History, 12; Yale Collections of Western Americana,
Beinecke Rare Book and Manuscript Library, 18, 20 (all), 28

Printed in Canada.
102014   008478FRS15

TABLE OF CONTENTS

A NOTE ABOUT PRIMARY SOURCES

Primary sources are newspaper articles, photographs, speeches, or other documents that were created during an event. They are great ways to see how people spoke and felt during that time. You'll find primary sources from the time of U.S. westward expansion throughout this book. Within the text, primary source quotations are colored red and set in italic type.

GO WEST, YOUNG MAN

Since the first European settlers arrived in Virginia and Massachusetts, Americans have been on the move. First they settled the 13 colonies ruled by the British. With the Revolutionary War (1775–1783), the American colonists drove the British out and formed states. But as more people came to America, farmland grew scarce. People began to look westward for more land and better opportunities. Westward expansion began in the early 1800s and continued until about 1890. By then the West was settled, and the United States of America stretched from coast to coast.

Newspaper editor Horace Greeley urged America's youth to look west. *"Fly, scatter through the country—go to the Great West,"* he wrote in *The New Yorker* in June 1837. Thousands took up the challenge. With the popular phrase *"Go west, young man"* echoing in their ears, they headed west.

Thousands of pioneers left their homes and traveled across the dangerous West in search of new lives.

Some went to find land where they could start farms. Others went for riches. Still others went looking for a home where they could worship freely.

But before any of these Americans could travel west, someone had to blaze a trail and show them the way. These were the explorers and adventurers.

EARLY EXPLORERS

Before 1800 France owned much of the western part of North America, known as the Louisiana Territory. French leader Napoleon Bonaparte offered to sell this huge region to the United States for $15 million. President Thomas Jefferson approved the sale in 1803. The Louisiana Purchase is one of the greatest land deals of all time. This purchase added about 828,000 square miles (2,144,000 square kilometers) of land to the United States. The nation doubled in size overnight.

No one knew what this new land looked like or who lived there. Jefferson sent an **expedition**, led by Meriwether Lewis and William Clark, to explore the territory all the way to the Pacific Ocean. For two years Lewis, Clark, and their party of about 40 explorers crossed the vast wilderness. They made contact with American Indian tribes, took notes on everything they saw, and collected samples of plants and animals.

expedition—a journey with a goal, such as exploring or searching for something

△ The Lewis and Clark expedition inspired many people to think about going west.

◁ from Lewis' journal, February 24, 1806

"... The Shallun or deep purple berry is in form much like the huckkleberry ... the stem or trunk is from three to 10 Inches in circumference irregularly ... the natives either eat these berrys when ripe immediately from the bushes or dried in the sun ..."

— from Lewis' journal January 26, 1806

The explorers returned home in 1806 and were praised as heroes. Their exploration of the West inspired other Americans to travel there.

THE MOUNTAIN MEN

Some of the young men who traveled with Lewis and Clark didn't return to the East with them. They remained in the wilderness to take up a new trade—fur trapping. They were soon joined by other adventurers. The fur of beavers and other animals was used to make men's hats and other fashionable clothes of the day. *"I started into the mountains with the determination of becoming a first-rate hunter ... and of making the whole profitable to me."* said Jedediah Smith.

These adventurous men crossed the Rocky Mountains in their hunt for furs. They came to be called "mountain men." Mountain men spent long stretches of time in the wilderness, trapping animals for fur. They also traded for furs with American Indian tribes. Some mountain men even lived with Indians and had Indian wives.

Painted by Jim Carson, this image shows mountain man John Colter (left) meeting the Blackfoot Indians while hunting for fur.

In their travels the mountain men discovered places that no white man had seen before. They went back east with tales of these wondrous places. Mountain man John Colter bragged about a region filled with *"hidden fires, smoking pits, noxious steams, and smell of brimstone."* Most people didn't believe his stories and called this place "Colter's Hell." Today it is known as Yellowstone National Park.

MANIFEST DESTINY

By 1840 beaver hats fell out of fashion, and the beaver trade began to fade. The day of the mountain men was ending. However, their reports of new lands convinced many Americans to head west. Some mountain men found new work leading wagon trains of pioneers westward on the very same trails they used for trapping.

Some people believed that the urge to move westward was more than a personal need. Many believed that spreading across the country was a duty given to Americans by God. This idea encouraged people to spread across the continent to establish a powerful nation.

Newspaper writer John O'Sullivan wrote an editorial in the *New York Morning News* in 1845, explaining the idea. He also gave the idea a name—**manifest destiny**. *"Away, away with all these cobweb tissues of rights of discovery, exploration, settlement ... our claim to Oregon would still be best and strongest. And that claim is by the right of our manifest destiny to overspread and to possess the whole of the continent which Providence [God] has given us ..."*

manifest destiny—the belief that God gave white Americans the right to take over lands that belonged to other people

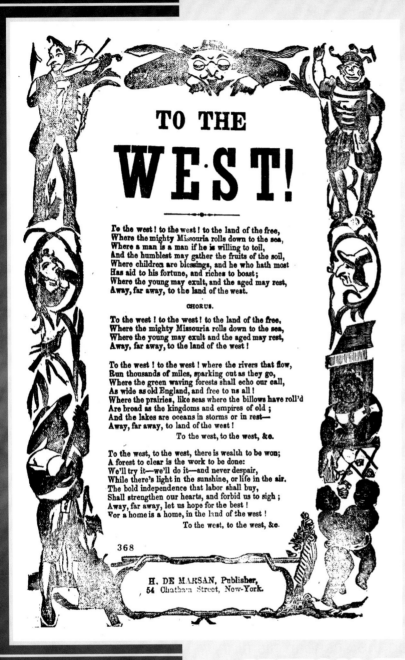

TO THE WEST!

To the west! to the west! to the land of the free,
Where the mighty Missouria rolls down to the sea,
Where a man is a man if he is willing to toil,
And the humblest may gather the fruits of the soil,
Where children are blessings, and he who hath most
Has aid to his fortune, and riches to boast;
Where the young may exult, and the aged may rest,
Away, far away, to the land of the west.

CHORUS.

To the west! to the west! to the land of the free,
Where the mighty Missouria rolls down to the sea,
Where the young may exult and the aged may rest,
Away, far away, to the land of the west!

To the west! to the west! where the rivers that flow,
Run thousands of miles, sparking out as they go,
Where the green waving forests shall echo our call,
As wide as old England, and free to us all!
Where the prairies, like seas where the billows have roll'd
Are broad as the kingdoms and empires of old;
And the lakes are oceans in storms or in rest—
Away, far away, to land of the west!
To the west, to the west, &c.

To the west, to the west, there is wealth to be won;
A forest to clear is the work to be done:
We'll try it—we'll do it—and never despair,
While there's light in the sunshine, or life in the air.
The bold independence that labor shall buy,
Shall strengthen our hearts, and forbid us to sigh;
Away, far away, let us hope for the best!
For a home is a home, in the land of the west!
To the west, to the west, &c.

368

H. DE MARSAN, Publisher,
54 Chatham Street, New-York.

◁ The movement to go west became so popular, many artists wrote songs about it. "To the West" shows the hope people had for the *"green waving forests"* and the trust that this open land would bring those who were willing to work a *"bold Independence."*

CRITICAL THINKING

The mountain men had lived and worked with American Indians living in the western lands of the United States. How would manifest destiny affect the relationships white people had with American Indians?

SETTLING TEXAS AND UTAH

By 1830 more than 20,000 Americans had moved into Mexican-owned Texas. The growing number of Americans there alarmed the Mexican government. It shut down further immigration to the area. The Americans didn't like the controlling Mexican government, so they formed their own army and government.

In early 1836 General Santa Anna, the Mexican leader, led a large army to San Antonio to take back the city. He attacked the Alamo, an old mission where about 200 Texan defenders were stationed. Texan leader Colonel William Travis wrote to the governor of Texas for reinforcements. *"... I am besieged, by a thousand or more of the Mexicans ... I call on you in the name of Liberty ... to come to our aid ..."*

But no reinforcements came, and the Alamo fell on March 6, 1836. José Juan Sánchez Navarro, a Mexican official, recorded the scene in his diary. Translated into English it said, *"Today at five in the morning, the assault was made by four columns ... By six-thirty there was not an enemy left ... Two hundred fifty-seven of their men were killed ..."*

TEXAS!!

Emigrants who are desirous of assisting Texas at this important crisis of her affairs may have a free passage and equipments, by applying at the **NEW-YORK and PHILADELPHIA HOTEL,** On the Old Levee, near the Blue Stores.

Now is the time to ensure a fortune in Land: To all who remain in Texas during the War will be allowed 1280 Acres. To all who remain Six Months, 640 Acres. To all who remain Three Months, 320 Acres. And as Colonists, 4600 Acres for a family and 1470 Acres for a Single Man.

New Orleans, April 23d, 1836.

Δ Posters, like this one from April 23, 1836, encouraged people to go to Texas during the war to make it harder for the Mexican army. Colonists who stayed were offered free land.

On April 21, 1836, a Texas army defeated Santa Anna at the Battle of San Jacinto. As the Texans fought, they cried *"Remember the Alamo!"* Texas independence was won. Excited about the Texans' success, more and more Americans came to settle in this independent republic.

Ten years later the United States went to war with Mexico over an argument about Texas' border. President James Polk was a deep believer in manifest destiny. Many believe Polk pushed the country into the Mexican War (1846–1848) to gain more land for the United States.

The United States won the war and took over areas previously under Mexican control. They included present-day California, Nevada, Utah, most of New Mexico and Arizona, and parts of Colorado and Texas. It proved to be the largest addition of land to the United States since the Louisiana Purchase.

◁ *The Fall of the Alamo* by Robert Jenkins Onderdonk, created in 1903

CRITICAL THINKING

Compare Travis' quotation with Navarro's. Why would the Texans use the memory of the Alamo as inspiration for further fighting?

GOING WEST FOR RELIGIOUS FREEDOM

Soon after becoming a U.S. possession, Utah was settled by the Mormons. This religious group had formed in New York. Many people disapproved of their religious beliefs and often verbally and physically attacked them. Thomas Sharp, editor of an anti-Mormon newspaper wrote in 1844, *"Citizens Arise, One and All!!!—Can you stand by, and suffer such infernal devils! to rob men of their property and rights, without avenging them. We have no time for comment, every man will make his own. Let it be Made with Powder and Ball."*

Many Mormons moved west, looking for a place to settle. Under the leadership of Brigham Young, a group of 148 Mormons arrived at the Salt Lake Valley in what is today Utah on July 24, 1847. When Young looked down on the valley he is supposed to have said, *"This is the right place!"* Not everyone in his party agreed with him. *"Weak and weary as I am,"* wrote Harriet Young in her diary, *"I would rather go a thousand miles farther than remain in such forsaken place as this."*

The Mormons called their new home Deseret, meaning honeybee. However, when the area became a territory in 1850, the U.S. government named it Utah after the Utes, a local American Indian tribe.

Mormons traveled through dangerous lands, such as the Echo Canyon in Utah, to reach a place to settle.

The valley was desolate, dry, and not good for growing anything. But under Young's leadership, Salt Lake City began to take shape. An **irrigation** system was created to bring water to the dry land from surrounding mountain streams. By 1865 the Mormons had built more than 1,000 miles (1,609 km) of canals to irrigate thousands of acres of farmland.

News of the Mormon colony spread back east and to Europe. Thousands of Europeans crossed the ocean and made the long journey to the Salt Lake Valley. Other Americans were inspired to go west by the Mormons' success in Utah.

irrigation—supplying water to crops using a system of pipes or channels

THE OREGON TRAIL

Few areas of the West were more appealing to settlers than the Willamette Valley of the Oregon Territory. This valley was full of **fertile** farmland and beautiful views.

The Oregon Trail that led to this earthly paradise was first laid out by the mountain men. The trail stretched 2,000 miles (3,219 km) from Independence, Missouri, to the Willamette Valley. Pioneers traveled along it in trains of about 15 covered wagons. The first wagon train arrived in Oregon in 1843. That year 1,000 pioneers made the trek. Two years later 3,000 travelers took the trip.

The trail was full of dangers. Travelers faced hot deserts, high mountains, diseases such as cholera, and **hostile** Indians. A death notice in the diary of a survivor notes the grim reality of life and death on the long journey.

"Jon A. Dawson, St. Louis, Mo.
Died Oct. 1, 1849
From eating a poisonous root
at the spring"

fertile—good for growing crops
hostile—unfriendly or angry

Pioneers buried those who died on the journey along the trail. Today crude grave markers, like this one for Lucinda E. Wright near South Pass, Wyoming, still dot the land as a reminder of the brave people who headed west.

NOT-SO-SHORTCUTS

Life on the trail was made more dangerous by misinformation. Many people offered tips and tricks for making it to Oregon faster. But some of their information was false.

In 1845 Lansford Hastings published a guide for pioneers traveling to California and Oregon. He mentioned a shortcut across Utah, "the Hastings Cutoff." But Hastings had not taken this shortcut when he wrote the guide. He had only learned about it from a report by an explorer doing a geographical survey.

One wagon train, led by George Donner, followed this shortcut. The path was terribly difficult and put the group behind schedule and short on food. The group reached the Sierra Nevada mountains in October and was stopped by a raging blizzard. The group of men, women, and children spent five months trapped in the mountains. Patrick Breen, one of the men trapped, wrote in his diary on December 17, 1846. *"... May we with Gods help spend the comeing year better than the past which we purpose to do if Almighty God will deliver us from our present dreadful situation ..."*

Only 46 of the original 87 party members survived.

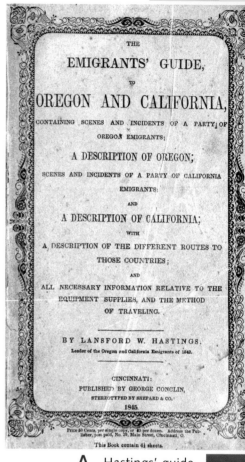

△ Hastings' guide

It wasn't all danger on the trail. The wagon trains had many good days and happy experiences. Wagon train captain Jesse Applegate's memories of quiet nights were published in the *Overland Monthly* magazine around 1876. *"It is not yet eight o'clock, when the first watch is to be set. The evening meal is just over ... near the river a violin makes lively music, and some youths ... have improvised a dance ... in another quarter a flute gives its mellow ... notes to the still night air ..."*

By 1848 more than 11,000 settlers had come to Oregon, and the region was officially organized into the Territory of Oregon. It became the 33rd state in 1859.

CALIFORNIA GOLD RUSH

While California had new settlers too, it did not experience the growth of Oregon until a remarkable event occurred.

On January 24, 1848, carpenter James Marshall was building a mill for landowner John Sutter on the American River in California. *"My eye was caught by something shining in the bottom of the ditch,"* Marshall later said. *"I reached my hand down and picked it up ... then I saw another."*

EL DORADO

OF THE

UNITED STATES OF AMERICA.

THE DISCOVERY

OF

INEXHAUSTIBLE GOLD MINES

IN

CALIFORNIA.

Tremendous Excitement among the Americans.

The Extensive Preparations

TO

MIGRATE TO THE GOLD REGION,

&c. &c. &c.

△ *The California Herald* newspaper printed a full page article on December 26, 1848, encouraging people to come to the "gold region."

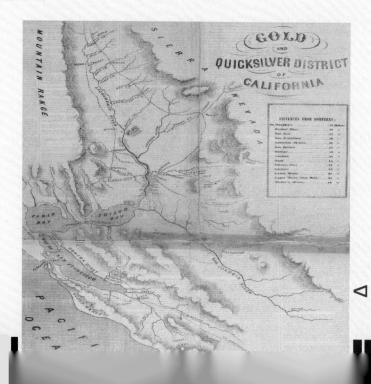

◁ The *Herald's* article included a map of the area for gold seekers.

Gold Region

Sacramento
San Francisco
ATLANTIC OCEAN
PACIFIC OCEAN
N W E S
ATLANTIC OCEAN
Strait of Magellan
Cape Horn

Scale
0 500 1,000 miles
0 500 1,000 kilometers

What Marshall found was gold. Word of the discovery soon swept through the region. Newspaper headlines brought thousands of gold seekers to California from the East and other countries. Many of these fortune hunters arrived in 1849 and came to be called the "49ers."

◁ The 49ers traveled by sea and across land to reach California.

James Marshall in front of Sutter's mill in about 1948 ▷

WINNERS AND LOSERS

Early discoveries of gold led many miners to think they would strike it rich. A popular song of the time supported this hope.

"Gold out there, and everywhere.
And everybody is a millionaire
You'll get rich quick by takin' up a pick,
And diggin' up a chunk as big as a brick."

Among the thousands who came for gold were Hawaiians and Chinese. The Chinese miners called America *Gum Shan*, "the Gold Mountain."

This photograph was taken in 1851 after the Maidu Indians signed a treaty with white leaders. American Indians signed many treaties with white leaders in California to protect their lands. However, most treaties were ignored, and the Indians were pushed off their lands by gold seekers.

Almost no women went to California to search for gold. In 1852 more than 90 percent of the gold miners were men.

gold miners by a sluice box in Aubine Ravine, California, around 1852

But there were no mountains of gold. Panning for gold was hard work. And few prospectors found much, if any, gold.

The biggest losers, however, were American Indians. Within a decade of the Gold Rush, as many as 100,000 of the 170,000 Indians living in California died from violence, diseases, and starvation. As one chief of the Nisenan people supposedly said, *"The spirit that owns the yellow metal is a bad spirit. It will drive you crazy if you possess it."*

The biggest winner in the Gold Rush was California itself. Before the gold rush began, the territory's white population was less than 15,000. By the end of 1849, more than 100,000 white people lived in California. It became the 31st state the following year.

SETTLING THE PLAINS

For many years the U.S. government owned much of the land in the western United States. Many citizens wanted that land to build their homes and farms on. Finally, in 1862, Congress passed the Homestead Act. According to this act, any citizen 21 years old could settle 160 acres (65 hectares) of western land. If settlers lived on the land for five years, it would be deeded to them. Over the next 38 years, up to 600,000 families moved into homesteads under the act.

The Homestead Act remained in force until 1976 in every state but Alaska. It continued in Alaska until 1986.

In 1868 Daniel Freeman was the first person to receive a deed for land he settled under the Homestead Act.

HOMESTEAD.

Land Office at *Brownville Neb*

January 20 1868.

CERTIFICATE, No. 1

APPLICATION, No. 1

It is hereby certified, That pursuant to the provisions of the act of Congress, approved May 20, 1862, entitled "An act to secure homesteads to actual settlers on the public domain," *Daniel Freeman* has made payment in full for *E½ of NW¼ of NE¼ of NW¼ and SW¼ of NE¼* of Section *Twenty Six (26)* in Township *four (4) N* of Range *five (5) E* containing *160* acres. Now, therefore, be it known, That on presentation of this Certificate to the COMMISSIONER OF THE GENERAL LAND OFFICE, the said *Daniel Freeman* shall be entitled to a Patent for the Tract of Land above described.

Henry M. Atkinson

Register.

Most of these homesteaders settled on the **Great Plains**, the last frontier of the United States to be settled. The plains earth was rich and fertile, but it was covered by hard **sod**. Farmers cut up the sod and used it to build their homes because there were no trees for wood. Sod homes were sturdy and cool in the hot summers and warm in the cold winters. But there were hazards to sod houses. Insects and snakes infested the walls. Sod roofs also had a tendency to leak when it rained. As one child of a sodbuster recalled in a memoir, "... *The long ridge pole on the roof began to crack from the heavy weight of the wet sod, and finally the roof caved in with the pole resting on the table. We were buried beneath the sod and the muck. Finally father saw a little patch of light and he dug his way out.*"

◁ a family in Nebraska in front of their sod house in 1886

Great Plains—the broad, level land that stretches eastward from the base of the Rocky Mountains for about 400 miles (644 km) in the United States and Canada

sod—the top layer of soil and the grass attached to it

HARD TIMES

Life on the plains for early pioneers was hard in many ways. Men worked the fields, and women cooked, cleaned, and raised children. It was also lonely. The pioneers had left their families and friends behind to start their new lives. One Kansas homesteader wrote in her diary, *"I saw a vast expanse of prairie country in sunset, but it looked so very lonesome, and so I cried, in a moment of longing for my family so far away."*

Many pioneers missed their old homes, but they adjusted to their new ones. This was not true for the American Indians who lived on the Great Plains. White settlers began building homes and towns where the Indians had once lived. To make sure white settlers could have the land, the U.S. military forced Indians west and **confined** them to **reservations**.

▷ Settlers on the plains used resources from the land to survive. Women, such as this one in Kansas in 1893, often collected buffalo chips, or poop, to burn as fuel to heat their homes.

△ a Lakota Indian camp near Pine Ridge Indian Reservation, in South Dakota, in 1891

"A long time ago this land belonged to our fathers;" said the Kiowa chief Santana, *"but when I go up to the river I see camps of soldiers here on its banks. These soldiers cut down my timber; they kill my buffalo; and when I see that, my heart feels like bursting; I feel sorry."*

CRITICAL THINKING

Compare the homesteader's diary entry with Santana's quotation. If those two people were able to talk to each other, would they have any similar feelings?

confine—to keep within certain bounds
reservation—an area of land set aside by the U.S. government for American Indians

FROM SEA TO SHINING SEA

On July 1, 1862, President Abraham Lincoln signed the Pacific Railroad Act. Two railroad companies were given the task of building a railroad that would unite the United States from coast to coast. On May 10, 1869, the two railroads met at Promontory Summit, Utah.

In 1869 photographer Andrew J. Russell captured the celebration held after completing the railroad.

The **transcontinental** railroad changed westward expansion forever. Crossing the West took four months in a covered wagon. On a train, it took a week to go from coast to coast. The railroad not only carried people west, but also supplies, food, and every other thing settlers needed.

transcontinental—extending or going across a continent

1869. May 10th. 1869.
GREAT EVENT
Rail Road from the Atlantic to the Pacific
GRAND OPENING
— OF THE —

Union Pacific

RAIL ROAD,

PLATTE VALLEY ROUTE.

PASSENGER TRAINS LEAVE

OMAHA

ON THE ARRIVAL OF TRAINS FROM THE EAST.

THROUGH TO SAN FRANCISCO
In less than Four Days, avoiding the Dangers of the Sea!

Travelers for Pleasure, Health or Business
Will find a Trip over The Rocky Mountains Healthy and Pleasant.

LUXURIOUS CARS & EATING HOUSES
ON THE UNION PACIFIC RAIL ROAD.

PULLMAN'S PALACE SLEEPING CARS
RUN WITH ALL THROUGH PASSENGER TRAINS.

GOLD, SILVER AND OTHER MINERS!
Now is the time to seek your Fortunes in Nebraska, Wyoming, Arizona, Washington, Dakotah Colorado, Utah, Oregon, Montana, New Mexico, Idaho, Nevada or California.

CONNECTIONS MADE AT

CHEYENNE for DENVER, CENTRAL CITY & SANTA FE
AT OGDEN AND CORINNE FOR HELENA, BOISE CITY, VIRGINIA CITY, SALT LAKE CITY AND ARIZONA.

THROUGH TICKETS FOR SALE AT ALL PRINCIPAL RAILROAD OFFICES.

Be Sure they Read via Platte Valley or Omaha

In 1891 superintendent of the census, Robert Porter, wrote, *"... there can hardly be said to be a frontier line."* Where once there had been a wilderness, there were now homes, farms, towns, and even cities.

People went west for many reasons. Some wanted to strike it rich in the California gold fields. Others were looking for a place where they could live in peace and prosper. The West met all their needs. The mass migration of Americans turned the United States from a small country of 13 states into a mighty nation stretching from Atlantic to Pacific.

◁ In 1869 railroad companies created posters advertising the new coast-to-coast line.

SELECTED BIBLIOGRAPHY

Breen, Patrick. The Diary of Patrick Breen. Online by PBS.
http://www.pbs.org/wgbh/americanexperience/features/primary-resources/donner-diary-patrick-breen/

Hampshire, Annette P. *Thomas Sharp and Anti-Mormon Sentiment in Illinois 1842–1845*. Online by Northern Illinois University Libraries' Historical Digitization Projects. http://dig.lib.niu.edu/ISHS/ishs-1979may/ishs-1979may082.pdf

Porter, Robert P. "Extra Census Bulletin No. 2. Washington D.C. April 20, 1891." Online by the Internet Archive. http://archive.org/stream/extracensusbulle00unit/extracensusbulle00unit_djvu.txt

Stewart, George R. *The California Trail: An Epic with Many Heroes*. New York: McGraw-Hill Book Company, Inc., 1962. Online by Internet Archive. https://archive.org/details/californiatraila013595mbp

Travis, William Barret. "Letter from the Alamo." February 24, 1836. Online by the Texas Heritage Society. http://texasheritagesociety.org/The-Travis-Letter-Victory-or-Death.html

Welsch, Roger L. "The Nebraska Soddy." *Nebraska History*, 1967. Online by Nebraska State Historical Society. http://www.nebraskahistory.org/publish/publicat/history/full-text/NH1967NE_Soddy.pdf

White, Richard. *It's Your Misfortune and None of My Own: A New History of the American West*. Norman, Okla.: University of Oklahoma Press, 1991.

The Young Woman's Journal. Salt Lake City: The Deseret News, 1909. http://books.google.com/books?id=qrIUAAAAYAAJ&printsec=frontcover&source=gbs_ge_summary_r&cad=0#v=onepage&q&f=false

GLOSSARY

confine (kuhn-FINE)—to keep within certain bounds

expedition (ek-spuh-DI-shuhn)—a journey with a goal, such as exploring or searching for something

fertile (FUHR-tuhl)—good for growing crops; fertile soil has many nutrients

Great Plains (GRAYT PLAYNS)—the broad, level land that stretches eastward from the base of the Rocky Mountains for about 400 miles (644 km) in the United States and Canada

hostile (HOSS-tuhl)—unfriendly or angry

irrigation (ihr-uh-GAY-shuhn)—supplying water to crops using a system of pipes or channels

manifest destiny (MAN-uh-fest DESS-tuh-nee)—the belief that God gave white Americans the right to take over lands that belonged to other people

reservations (rez-er-VAY-shuhn)—an area of land set aside by the U.S. government for American Indians

sod (SOD)—the top layer of soil and the grass attached to it

transcontinental (transs-kon-tuh-NEN-tuhl)—extending or going across a continent

INTERNET SITES

FactHound offers a safe, fun way to find Internet sites related to this book. All of the sites on FactHound have been researched by our staff.

Here's all you do:

Visit *www.facthound.com*

Type in this code: 9781491418413

 **Super-cool stuff!** Check out projects, games and lots more at **www.capstonekids.com**

INDEX